# WATCHING FROM THE BLEACHERS

*poems by*

# Eileen Ivey Sirota

*Finishing Line Press*
Georgetown, Kentucky

# WATCHING FROM THE BLEACHERS

Copyright © 2024 by Eileen Ivey Sirota
ISBN 979-8-88838-608-8 First Edition
All rights reserved under International and Pan-American Copyright Conventions. No part of this book may be reproduced in any manner whatsoever without written permission from the publisher, except in the case of brief quotations embodied in critical articles and reviews.

## ACKNOWLEDGMENTS

Grateful acknowledgments to the following literary journals where some of the poems in this book have appeared:

"Springtime 1349, Springtime 2020," "Watching from the Bleachers," and "The Calendar Refuses to Perform its Function" are reprinted with permission of *Voices: The Art and Science of Psychotherapy and the American Academy of Psychotherapists*
"Whitewash," "Front Lines," and "In Which I Interrogate My Frequent Response" were originally published by *New Verse News*
"Disclosed," "The Employment of African Americans in Agriculture," and "Landscape with the Fall of Icarus" were originally published by *The Ekphrastic Review*
"Our House" was originally published in *The Poeming Pigeon*

With appreciation for my many fellow-travelers in poetry who have provided encouragement, inspiration, and critique: Ellen Cole, Mary Kay Schoen, Jaime Banks, Kim Roberts, Teri Ellen Cross Davis, Sandra Beasley and others.

To Terrance Hayes, a double debt of gratitude for his fierce and potent work and his invention of the Golden Shovel form which often inspires me when nothing else can. I owe the title of this book to him.

With gratitude to Linda Kanefield, my most supportive and steadfast early reader.

Thanks to Carol Kranowitz for generous consultation, editing and hilarity.

To life its own damn self, the grit within the pearl, for providing inspiration and irritation.

For Rachel and Len, whose love sustains me, no words are sufficient.


Publisher: Leah Huete de Maines
Editor: Christen Kincaid
Cover Art and Design: Rachel Sirota
Author Photo: 1250 Productions


Order online: www.finishinglinepress.com
  also available on amazon.com

Author inquiries and mail orders:
Finishing Line Press
PO Box 1626
Georgetown, Kentucky 40324
USA

# Contents

I.

Watching from the Bleachers ................................................................. 2
Whitewash ................................................................................................. 3
Turning Over the Keys ............................................................................ 4
The New "New Colossus" ....................................................................... 5
Our House ................................................................................................. 6
In Which I Interrogate My Frequent Response .................................. 7
Front Lines ................................................................................................ 8
Disclosed ................................................................................................... 9
Rise Up .................................................................................................... 10

II.

Springtime 1349, Springtime 2020 ..................................................... 12
The First Month ..................................................................................... 13
Covid Time .............................................................................................. 14
The Calendar Refuses to Perform Its Function ................................ 15
Master Class ............................................................................................ 16
Advice to a Freshman ........................................................................... 17
Awakening 1967 ..................................................................................... 18
The Urban Dictionary: Guide to a Delicate Dialect ........................ 19
The Drey .................................................................................................. 20
Who Doesn't Love a—? ........................................................................ 21
Generations ............................................................................................. 22
Rinsed Spaghetti .................................................................................... 23
Two Hungers ........................................................................................... 24
Elder Sex ................................................................................................. 26

III.

The poem about my mother is the poem that will not write itself ........... 28
Unsolved ................................................................................................. 29
Landscape with the Fall of Icarus ....................................................... 30
The Presence of Absent Things ........................................................... 31
Gone ........................................................................................................ 32
In my dreams I could do anything ..................................................... 33
Pilgrim Lake ........................................................................................... 34

# I.

*"Art is not a mirror held up to reality but a hammer with which to shape it."*
*Bertolt Brecht*

*"He is the best friend of this country who dares tell his countrymen the truth."*
*Frederick Douglass*

## Watching from the Bleachers

*A Golden Shovel after Terrance Hayes' "I lock you in an American sonnet that is part prison" from American Sonnets for My Past and Future Assassin*

Here we are—still and always: two Americas. While
others drive the screaming ambulances, deliver your
groceries, debate whether sleeping in the car would be better
than subjecting their kids to their exposed and worried selves,

you sit before Netflix recovering from a day of Zoom or watch
new episodes of Black History programming from
PBS and think about replacing the
earrings you dropped last year under the bleachers.

## Whitewash

All the white pages lovely, unspoiled
by time, untouched by torment.
All aboard.

An uninterrupted arc of progress.
Heroes on horseback. See Dick and Jane
in their triumphant ignorance.

We have torn you
from our history books, those fairy tales
for innocents and children.

Unseen and unheard are the children we ripped
from their mothers, sent away
to boarding schools to be laundered
and whitened, their mother tongue ripped out.

*"Kill the Indian and save the man"* proclaimed Lt. Col. Pratt.
In Pennsylvania, one hundred eighty-six graves
cradle their small bones.

From your mouths we tore
the sacred place names and stamped them
on our suburban street signs.

So many ways of killing—the bullet, the blanket,
the exile, the pretending, the silence.
The silence.

**Turning Over the Keys**

*On the occasion of the Presidential Inauguration January 20, 2021*
*With thanks to Gil Scott Heron, "The Revolution Will Not Be Televised"*

The shine is off the American buggy,
the paint is peeling, the tires slump,
the shocks have suffered our shock

at cars plowing fields of peaceful protesters.
The city on the hill has been trampled,
corrupted, shit-smeared.

Again and again we learn:
it was always so.

Barbarians literally at the gate.
It turns out the revolution
actually will be televised.

What alchemy can make wisdom from lies?
Unity from hatred? One more time
we put the key in the ignition and listen—
straining to hear a faint, hopeful hum.

## The New "New Colossus"

> *"Why do we want all these people from 'shithole countries' coming here?"*
> Jan. 12, 2018, Donald Trump opining about his least preferred immigrants

Give me your folks who rape and maul,
your huddled masses yearning to live for free,
the refuse of your shitholes large and small.
Send these, the homeless, tempest-tossed to me—
I'll kick their ass back o'er our golden wall.

**Our House**

we live in the most flawless house
spotless and spacious, as lavish
as ever you could wish

it's been in our family for generations
birthed victors and champions
unbreakable traditions

we never go down to the basement

the names are stuffed in the basement
Rayshard, George, Breonna, Ahmaud, Philando,
Sandra, Freddie, Tamir, Michael, Eric, Trayvon

the souvenirs are tossed in the basement
postcards mugs and magnets from Atlanta,
Minneapolis, Louisville, Georgia, Minnesota,
Texas, Baltimore, Cleveland, Ferguson, Staten Island, Florida

in the basement are the shouts and whispers
*Hands up don't shoot*
*I can't breathe*
and the bodies, strong and broken

there are no lights in the basement—
that way we can't see

**In Which I Interrogate My Frequent Response**

what can grow
in this salty pool

that does not bring back
a single Emmett or Ahmaud

that does not cleanse
so much as one tainted tree

this sterile balm

useless as nipples on a tomcat:
white woman tears

## Front Lines

> *On April 8, 2022, the governor of Alabama signed into law two controversial bills: one that criminalizes healthcare providers who offer gender-affirming care to transgender youth and another that requires students to use bathrooms that match the gender on their birth certificates.*

We will fight them on the
beaches. We will fight them

in the sandbox. These tiny
terrorists, the little boys

with nail polish, a spangly pony
and a special Barbie.

We have God on our side—
He who surely must have sanctified

the hand of the doctor filling out
the birth certificate. We have

George Orwell on our side
who daily inspires our marketing team.

We'll call it de-nazification, no,
we'll call it parental support, no,

wait, we'll call it The Vulnerable Child
Compassion and Protection Act.

No more shelter in the demilitarized
school nurse's office. We'll make it a crime

to pause the ordained march of puberty,
to delay the emergence of the prescribed

body. In this holy war
no prisoners are too small.

**Disclosed**

    (after Kizito Maria Kasule's painting *Togetherness*)

Naked, transparent, exposed,
she is the very portrait
of white fragility.

She begs: *Why can't
I have some clothes,
or a loincloth, at the least?
When someone speaks of race,
I am uncovered
how I profit from the sins*

*of my father and forefathers,
from the tilt of our laws,
the shape of our neighborhoods.*

She implores us to drape her
in some camouflage—
perhaps a law to ban

the examination of history,
that unflinching x-ray machine
into our secret heartwood.

Kizito Maria Kasule, *Togetherness*
CC BY-SA 4.0

**Rise Up**

*after Earle Richardson's painting Employment of African-Americans in Agriculture*

It is 1934—the rows of cotton, deceptively beautiful,
are endless, the landscape warm and round,
the sun relentless. The workers rise up

straight with strength and grit, though surely
their backs must ache and hands cramp
after hours imprisoned by their labor.

Perhaps the artist sensed his title was a pleasing lie
for the Federal Art Project—"employment" a fig leaf
for the new slavery of sharecropping.

Or perhaps, born in the North, the artist borrowed courage
from his unbreakable brothers and sisters
still toiling in the South.

And now it is 1935. Unseen in this painting, the painter,
Earle Richardson, only twenty-three, has been left alone
in a hard and angular universe by the death of his lover

and collaborator. He opens the window and steps into the frigid
New York December. The dirty pavement, four stories below,
rises up to meet him.

Earle Richardson, *Employment of Negroes in Agriculture*
Smithsonian American Art Museum,
Transfer from the U.S. Department of Labor, 1964.
public domain

II.

"Lately, it occurs to me what a long, strange trip it's been."
The Grateful Dead

**Springtime 1349, Springtime 2020**

The earth still goes about her business.
The cherry blossoms still shed
their viral load of ephemeral elegance. The magnolias
still release the sweet scent of cyclical eternity.

The squirrels, who have not heard
of social distancing,
still make the thin dogwood branches dance
as they practice their springtime Olympics.

Inside: an abundance of caution.
Outside: an explosion of reckless abundance.

The oblivious beauty of the world
mocks us, comforts us.

## The First Month

when a passing car was a spectral rarity
when house finches sang brilliant solos against the stilled sky

when jokes careened manically from person to person
when through our windows we first saw the world's
infinite variety and fundamental sameness

when a virus bound us
in a web of wonder, fear and fellow-feeling

**Covid Time**

Stuck inside.
Nowhere to go.

Leaden time has stopped
like an old dog refusing to walk,

prostrate in the street.
The bed upstairs beckons.

Lying in your arms I remember
that afternoon in Athens

as we lay
atop the humid sheets

littered with pistachio shells from our feast,
sensations merging—soft, salty, sharp.

Later, I become again
an infant in my crib—

no toys but fingers, toes
and the sweet geometry

of sunlight peeking through the blinds,
dancing on the ceiling.

**The Calendar Refuses to Perform its Function**

That yammering magpie on the kitchen wall
has fallen silent. No more bossy,
officious black scribbles in overflowing

boxes. Suddenly she has
nothing to tell us about next Friday,
or even the third week in April.

Nothing to light the way.

No "dinner with Linda and Norm,"
no "usher at Arena Stage."
Only a succession of empty, waiting boxes.

**Master Class**

How even after seventeen lonely, horny years in darkness,
he is still a gentleman.
How he inclines his every sense to detect, above his racket
and that of his billion-strong fraternity—her click
of consent.

I see them tail to tail on the suburban blacktop.
How eager they must be
after their years of isolation and deprivation,
denied even a dream of sunshine,
to conclude *why don't we do it in the road?*

Less courteous
were the seventeen-year-olds I met in college.
How in lieu of tymbals wooing at 96 decibels, they courted
with threats of impending frigidity, with sulky comparisons to Mitch,
the freshman next door, *"who gets it every night."*

How even a short-lived insect can give
a master class in grace.

**Advice to a Freshman**

In the tropical funk of the college laundry room,
the grungy stranger eyed me with naked appraisal.
Slinging his graying underwear into the battered dryer

with the unmistakable confidence
of a senior, he threw out his best pick-up line—
*"Like who you are, but don't get too used to it."*

        A wiser fellow
        might have added:

Don't finish, never gel,
embrace the life of a dilettante.
Be, perhaps, in your 40s a potter,

in your 50s a quilter, in your 60s
a poet. Let seeming shyness
blossom into raging exhibitionism.

Save for the later years
the fresh pleasures of juggling and unicycling.
Discover a talent for holding the hands of the dying.

**Awakening 1967**

*A golden shovel poem after Leonard Cohen's "Hallelujah"*

That Ohio July, your voice on my scratchy record player, I
felt the quiver of every cell, newly birthed; fancied I could
bewitch you like half-crazy Suzanne, a perfect union not

only of body but mind, feel
the contours of your unmapped desires without so
much as a whisper or a whiff of shame. I

was the vibrating wire beneath the birds outside. Had you tried
to tell me I would someday be a septuagenarian, relegated to
silvered memory, I would have laughed, stilled your lips with a touch.

## The Urban Dictionary: Guide to a Delicate Dialect

*feel some kind of way*
        as if anger, like Voldemort, dare not be named

*friends with benefits*
        though one can search forever and not get vision
        and dental

*hook up*
        aspiring to the clean mechanical ease of Ikea
        assembly

*caught feelings*
        something a hat and muffler did not prevent
        and no amount of penicillin can cure

**The Drey**

The squirrels, cheeky
with nuts and with daring,

have pilfered
a pillow

and deconstructed it
into fluffy fibrous balls.

I watch one reassembling it,
in the oak tree fifty feet up.

This furry porter does not schlep;
her ascent is gravity-less and swift.

As recycler, aerialist
and parent, she is

tireless. In Spring, her kittens,
all unaware, will open their eyes

to a plush comfort
usually found only at the Ritz.

**Who Doesn't Love a—?**

elegant, expansive, evoking
the eternal, equipoised between
the spoken—and unspoken—

how humbly it welcomes
invisible possibilities
into its narrow bed

even upside down, it is still itself
a modest mark bearing the bulk of hope

Emily loved it—
the unseen more—

Zen master of punctuation:
em dash

**Generations**

The Russian dolls stand on the mantel,
one inside another inside another,

in all their fecund, female splendor. Smug,
with rosy cheeks, identical smiles,

bright peasant aprons tied over unfailing
generation-making bellies. Not a worry

in their babushka-ed heads about where
it all ends, they march without end

into their maternal future
from their maternal past.

But she who stands and regards them
feels like an empty doll,

chewing the gristle of grievance.
No doll ever nestled inside her,

nor in her daughter—imported from
another set—who cannot nest another.

**Rinsed Spaghetti**

When I was little, we had a tradition—
pasta was made, then sauced,
then the sauce rinsed off just for me.

I liked it better that way,
even better than plain,
how a distant note of the sauce remained.

Years later, across a conference table,
vast and cold as the table in *Citizen Kane*,
I stared at my soon-to-be ex—

his once-voluptuous mouth a knife's edge
in a granite jaw—and, unbidden, caught
a trace of the face I'd devoured by firelight

on our honeymoon in the Serengeti—
something soft in his eyes,
the tentative tilt of the head.

**Two Hungers**

        i.

These are the days of icily closed doors,
shouts and doubts,
*can't, won't* and *don't.*

But once there was no space between us.
Newly hatched from our cocoon,
I was *Mommy with the black hair*—

how you pressed me to agree
that once upon a time I must have been,
like you, a blonde.

No less than you I delighted in oneness.
Your hands patted my soft, permed hair;
my hands sought the velvet of your skin.

So many nights your small hands,
surprisingly strong, grasped my arm
to stay my nightly departure: *"don't go."*

Once those bedtime goodnights
seemed interminable,
everlasting.

        ii.

It sounded like a No
to me. Certainly less
than *let's*! You
beamed a furrowed brow
and I forgot delight,
penned in
mute exile.

So many nights my
hope lay in your hands
as I sought
to discover the

secrets of velvet
communion, receive the redemption of
your kiss, feast on the salt of your
skin.

**Elder Sex**

when you reached for me
across our soft, worn sheets
on the day before my birthday

I thought *"the dear old goat,*
*he just wants to sleep*
*with a young gal of 71 one last time!"*

with something lost perhaps in dexterity,
we continue to explore the syntax of skin,
the lexicon of longing.

III.

"I am half inclined to think we are all ghosts."
Henrik Ibsen, *Ghosts*, Act II

**The poem about my mother is the poem that will not write itself**

Shall I tell you how she wore a blue sweater
with pearls suspended along the edge of its satin collar,
and seemed to my six-year-old eyes

the most beautiful of women?
Or start with the image, puzzling but indelible,
of her tending to the Haitian janitor

after an aerosol can exploded
in his face—the same mother whose practical
nursing skills were overwhelmed

by the bleeding paw of my cat, Charlie Brown?
Or tell of her unrequited wish that I, her only child,
be her best friend? And how my sullen,

tight-lipped return from school defeated her daily?
Can I expunge the terrible years
when a world turned incomprehensible

made her mean? How she told a gleeful tale
(I still won't believe it)
of having secretly banished my beloved cat

for the crime of scratching the new porch screens?
And yet a time came when a simplified tranquility
descended and—though she remembered neither

my marriage nor my daughter—from across the room her radar
could spot my new high heels, my two-pound weight loss,
and her face would light with love.

**Unsolved**

One bench
two small boys in baseball uniforms
three skinned knees

On the bench the younger boy smiles up shyly—
a trusting Princess Diana smile—
from beneath his Buster Brown bangs

His big brother
glances at the photographer
with a sour, melancholic look—

at six he looks defeated.
His protective arm hangs limply
across my father's narrow shoulder

Sixty years later, my daughter, aged three,
sees the photo, concludes:
*"Uncle Thayer wants to cry."*

Ninety-five years later, they sit silently
astride my jewelry box—challenging me
to unravel the riddles of their natures,
their locked up secrets. Solve for x.

## Landscape with the Fall of Icarus

*(after William Carlos Williams and Bruegel's painting by that name)*

Most days I would tell you I feel like the peasant
scratching his ass at the bottom of Bruegel's painting,
humming perhaps,
perhaps thinking of the apple in his pocket.

But once I felt as Bruegel must have—
that attention must be paid.
It was the day in March my first parent died,
the day my father died.

Rushing across the street to the assisted living,
cell phone in hand, spreading my news,
unreality increasing with each retelling,
an ordinary, faceless day turned singular.

Unconcerned, the children and nannies in the park
played around the fountain, workers from nearby offices
carelessly tossed away their sandwich wrappings.
Daffodils elbowed their way hopefully through the thawing earth.

Pieter Brueghel, *Landscape with the Fall of Icarus*
public domain

### The Presence of Absent Things

*(For Jan, 1948—2005)*

I channel you in the incontinence aisle,
where we would have plotted an ad campaign
for elder diapers.

Octogenarians on horseback
would brandish canes with mock ferocity,
eyes twinkling roguishly from behind their specs,

while just across the aisle the other boxes
would sport plump toddlers crawling
towards global exploration.

*The Pampers baby—*
*why not the Depends dowager?*
I would have asked you.

**Gone**

> *"Who'll be my role model now that my role
> model is gone, gone?"*
> From *"You Can Call Me Al"* Paul Simon

Our fathers
were the first to go.

Ira did not complain.
A call from the hospital,
an hour later, another call.
*"Dad's gone."* No goodbyes.

Then Jack. Confused, dignity snatched,
yet still he released his last breath lightly,
a feather ascending to the heaven
he never believed in.

Then came the small mothers
who made hardly
a bump or ripple
beneath their covering sheets.

Hilda pulled slowly away from the shore,
drew breath, began to take another, then
reconsidered. Her hopeful last words:
*"I'll have another lamb chop."*

My Ruthie was last.
She slipped away with no one
there to hold her hand, smooth her hair.
Bereft even of the knowledge

of her widowhood,
she could only imagine
that another girlfriend
kept her husband from her side.

**in my dreams I could do anything**

swim with piglets
sing at La Scala
swap secrets with the Queen

bed Baryshnikov
Obama
or both

seed the bellies of
old women
with blooming pregnancies

and yet here I am again
visited nightly by my old familiars

my mother grins
as she does a mad fast shuffle
down the hallway of Brighton Gardens
to greet me in her unbuttoned blouse

my father catches my eye
struggles to rise from his wheelchair
in a gesture of approval (or silent censure?)

compelling me
to extend their muted half-life
for one more night

**Pilgrim Lake**

Seduced by first light, sleep's appeal
a distant dream, I slip out onto the deck.

Greedily I quaff the breeze,
a marriage of pine and brine.

My paddle neatly slices
shimmering pine trees.

Aging muscles remember
their green adolescence.

Dragonflies perform
an iridescent mating dance.

A wedding canopy of clouds
swirls like Florentine end papers.

Spiders weave seamless connections,
link branch to sill, join gutter to grill.

A toad seeks companionship
in my outdoor shower.

Great egrets confer on Mecca Island, wave
white handkerchief wings to declare peace,

their couriers dispatched back and forth
across the lake, spreading good news.

**Eileen Ivey Sirota** is a psychotherapist, poet, and potter. Her poems have appeared in *Calyx, District Lines, Beltway Poetry Quarterly, Voices: Journal of the American Academy of Psychotherapists, NewVerseNews, Ekphrastic Review, Lighten Up Online* and elsewhere. Her first chapbook, *Out of Order*, was published by Finishing Line Press. Having been raised in a family of political junkies and activists in the Washington DC area, political and cultural issues infuse her poetry. She lives in Bethesda, Maryland where she alternates between sputtering outrage and gobsmacked wonder. *Watching from the Bleachers* unites these two tendencies.

www.ingramcontent.com/pod-product-compliance
Lightning Source LLC
Chambersburg PA
CBHW040308170426
43194CB00022B/2937